DROPSHIPPING

Escape the 9-5 and Live Like A Rockstar

Gonçalo Hoshi

Copyright © 2018 (Gonçalo Hoshi)

All rights to this book are reserved. No permission is given for any part of this book to be reproduced, transmitted in any form or means; electronic or mechanical, stored in a retrieval system, photocopied, recorded, scanned, or otherwise. Any of these actions require the proper written permission of the publisher.

Disclaimer

All erudition contained in this book is given for informational and educational purposes only. The author is not in any way accountable for any results or outcomes that emanate from using this material. Constructive attempts have been made to provide information that is both accurate and effective, but the author is not bound for the accuracy or use/misuse of this information.

ISBN: 9781980361749

Copyright © 2018 Gonçalo Hoshi

Contents

SECTION ONE 5
    Mind Your Own Business 5
SECTION TWO 10
    What Is Drop-shipping 10
SECTION THREE 14
    How Drop-Shipping Works: The Process 14
SECTION FOUR 16
    Starting A Drop-Shipping Business 16
SECTION FIVE 25
    The Pros and Cons of Drop-Shipping 25
        The Pros of Drop-shipping 25
        The Cons of Drop-shipping 27
    CONCLUSION 30

SECTION ONE

Mind Your Own Business

We live in a world and time where having a single source of income just doesn't cut it anymore. In the same vein, if you decide to get a good job and earn monthly income, you might soon come to realize that this does not suffice and may not even be worth it. The boss at your workplace will work your ass out all through the month and then squeeze nuts into your pocket at the end of the month. An income which is hardly enough to settle the transport bills to work let alone pay the bills back at home. For how long will one rely on those peanuts?

I once saw a picture with the caption, "My boss bought a new Lamborghini and drove it to work, I congratulated him and told him just how nice the car was. My boss responded and said, 'If you work hard enough this year, I will buy another Lamborghini.'"

He isn't wrong now, is he? Here is the lesson I learned from that caption: Regardless of how hard you work for a boss, your hard work gets the boss wealthier and you, if not careful, poorer.

Now don't get me wrong, I am not by any means encouraging laziness, NO! Not to any degree, you need to be hard at work, the attitude you show to the work of others will to a large extent determine your attitude towards that which is yours.

But my point here is simple: MIND YOUR OWN BUSINESS!! These are words borrowed from the famous author Robert Kiyosaki in the book, "Rich Dad, Poor Dad." That statement cannot be less accurate. You just have to mind your own business! In other words, as we have established, working for others or having a sole source of income can't guarantee the financial independence that you so desire. However, if you take time to create your business world, and give your resources and effort to it, you are just on the path of financial greatness.

I know the thought that goes through your mind now will probably be, *what business do I have the know-how? Even if I do know one, am I just going to quit my job now? I have no prior savings, and it takes time to grow a business.*

Permit me to answer to your questions and thoughts one after the other starting from the last.

So, you have no prior savings and the it takes time to grow a business? Yes, that is true, but what you probably don't know is that there are businesses that you can start without having to open a shop or even stock up with goods, all you need is a virtual (online) shop. Yes! You heard that right. We live in a global online village you know; the internet has made many things that were impossible in the last century possible today.

You can be an online retailer having all sorts of exotic products in your shop without having to spend a dime acquiring the products. All you need do is discover the product needed by people, identify the product that picks your interest to sell, display your goods on your virtual shop, and when a prospective customer finds your store, simply link up with the manufacturer. The customer pays while the manufacturer ships the product to the consumer. You get paid in cash. A retail trade of this nature is possible because most manufacturers do not have the time and space to search out consumers; you can always fill that void and make your money. Business could be that simple!

So, do you have to quit your job? That's a risk I won't advise you take for now, at least not until you have complete financial independence. However, you can still keep your job and mind your own business anyway. It boils down to identifying the right "passive business."

While the phrase, "passive business" may be new to some, some might have heard about it before. So, what is a passive business? It's quite simple. It is a business you do that requires less of your attention and time. Unlike your job in which you are responsible to a boss, and you are expected to be actively involved during working hours and sometimes during the weekends, passive business requires little of your attention. Which means when you are not there, when you are busy attending to your active job, your passive business is running simultaneously and unhindered.

You need to know also that until you unlock the secret to a passive business and you build multiple streams of income from it, you're not yet on your way to wealth. The billionaires of our world today recognize the importance of passive business. So, they build most of their businesses to be passive, hence you see them play golf all day yet, there account booms with millions of dollars. They make money while in the toilet. Damn! That's just crazy, isn't it?

Now to our last question, you don't have the know-how about any business. Worry less about this because that is why I am here to introduce and teach you an idea that answers our three (3) curiosities. That is, a business that is rewarding with a requirement for little or zero start-up capital. What's more exciting? It is a passive but highly lucrative business.

Allow me to introduce you to DROP-SHIPPING! It is the complete package, but I know you have probably not heard about it before, that's why am going to take time out in the subsequent sections to explain what it is. How drop-shipping works, its pros and cons (you need to know this too), and how you can begin the drop-shipping business and passively make some cash for yourself.

SECTION TWO

What Is Drop-shipping

The increasing popularity of the internet has generated numerous career opportunities. Several businesses and industries abound on the web; the question is which one is feasible and viable?

Among numerous others, one thriving business I have discovered is drop-shipping. To describe simply, drop-shipping is a retail strategy that makes it possible for people to retail goods from anywhere to anywhere. In other words, drop-shipping allows any interested retailer around the world to contact manufacturers worldwide and get goods that he can sell to interested consumers, using the internet as the platform for transactions.

Traditionally, to start a retail business, you need to open up a shop or mart, with start-up capital, contact manufacturers, buy from them to stock up your store and then wait for buyers or consumers (who may never come in or to time) to patronize your goods in a cyclic style. On the other hand, drop-shipping can be done without going through the hassles of the traditional methods of retail trading.

The virtual business of drop-shipping is entirely viable nowadays as new products are being developed and manufactured at an incredibly faster rate than before. These manufacturers usually need a middleman retailer, who can get their products to consumers faster and more effectively.

Although numerous retailers exist with their shops in different parts of the world, these retailers are limited by a lot of things. First is the restriction that they have in time and space. In other words, a retail shop located on the streets of Detroit Michigan can only sell to consumers from the same area. In economics, such stores are described to have a limited market. *Secondly,* these stores run the risk of having outdated or expired goods. The need to pay rent, wages to staff, and taxes are other reasons why these retailers are limited.

With drop-shipping all these risks are eliminated, the manufacturer produces his goods, the retailer from the comfort of his room attracts customers, the customers get the products ordered and shipped down to a preferred address, the manufacturer is happy, the retailer is satisfied, the consumer is happy, everyone is happy!!!

Thus, drop-shipping is an arrangement between a business retailer and the manufacturer or distributor of a product. The retailer shows a desire and interest to sell the manufacturer's product on his behalf. The retailer creates an online store that doubles as an advertisement place, and interested consumers contact the retailer, who in turn inform the manufacturer. The manufacturer or distributor--and not the retailer--ships the product to the business's customers.

This means that it is a retail strategy in which a shop does not keep the products it sells in stock. When the store sells a product, it purchases it from the manufacturer or distributor who ships them directly to the customer. Drop-shipping allows the business to sell quality, brand name products online for a substantial profit, while the distributor or manufacturer looks after product development and order delivery.

So, if you are in the drop-shipping business, your role is that of a retailer who through prior notice to the manufacturer lists specific products on your internet platform for consumers to see. When consumers contact you, all you need do is contact the manufacturer in turn. The manufacturer then ships the product to the consumer. All you're doing is to provide information, connect the manufacturer to the consumer and get paid in the process.

SECTION THREE

How Drop-Shipping Works: The Process

Drop-shipping is a supply chain management business. In other words, the manufacturer has a supply to make, and the consumer has a demand for goods, while you're a middle man in the deal. The drop-shipping business fills the gap by linking market demand with supply and vice versa.

Through drop-shipping, the retailer partners with wholesale suppliers and distributors. This partnership enables the retailer to deliver online orders to the manufacturer or distributor directly. It becomes the duty of the manufacturer to ship the goods or products to the customer, while in the process pays the retailer (you) an agreed sum.

Let me explain in another way: when a drop-shipper receives a purchase order from a client, customer or buyer, the drop-shipper transfers information from the client to the distributor together with the shipping information. For instance; you are in a drop-shipping agreement with a phone manufacturing company. All you need do is create an online store, where you display the various types of products from the manufacturer. You can even have products for more than a single manufacturer on your page. Consumers perusing and looking for similar products will contact you. Your task will be to get their information and billing address, send same to the manufacturer. The distributor or wholesaler then ships the products directly to the customer. Most of the time, drop-shipping wholesalers include the retailer's name, logo and contact information with the product.

That is so cool, right? Yes, it is cool and it even more refreshing when your account starts booming with those currencies. However, to be successful with the drop-shipping business, you have specific actions to take, and that is what we will be discussing in the next section.

Let us try and answer the question you have in mind now. If my guess is right, you want to know what it takes to start, right?

SECTION FOUR

Starting A Drop-Shipping Business

Now, as you must have noticed thus far, the business of drop-shipping is not a magic that happens at the slightest wave of your hands. As much as it is a passive venture that requires little time, effort and almost zero cost, it still requires a deliberate and conscious attempt or action to succeed at it. Just like every other venture we engage in, we must put knowledge into action. So, in this section, I present to you step by step basics to starting and making money from the drop-shipping business.

STEP 1; Research the Product You Want to Sell

As simple as this step may sound, it is a very crucial one. In fact, the level of patronage you get which consequently determines the amount of money you make hinges on how well you get this step right. I have mentioned earlier that business is all about meeting the needs of people. Hold that rule dare in any business you want to do. Ask yourself these two ultimate and straightforward questions, "What do people need?" and "What competition exists for the retail of the good?"

It is advisable that the product you intend to sell is one that is in demand and at the same time not widely available on the web. While the second question might be the less important, the first is very crucial. The choice of good you are willing to sell must have a global demand, not just locally. Having a global market means that your customers are worldwide and are not limited to a group, class, state or country. If you allow this limitation in demand, you will end up defining your customer base and ultimately your income.

Once you make a list of high-demand goods, you might want to check the product with the least number of sellers. However, this counts for little because regardless of the number of sellers on a particular good, you are still sure to sell if you get your strategies right, especially given that it is a highly demanded good.

I mean, we are in a world of over 6 billion people! If you sell a good required by even half of that population (3 billion) and there are 10 thousand suppliers already, let's do the Maths, you have over 300,000 customers to one person. If you ask me, I will say that's huge!

Furthermore, when choosing a product to sell, do so with the brain and not the heart. What do I mean? That I have a personal preference for necklace doesn't mean the whole world does. I may love Samsung products, but the question is how many more people share my taste? This is business, jettison sentiments and be pragmatic. Never chose a product to sell just because you feel it is beautiful. Your choice of goods should be based on an in-depth market survey; which answers the question, "What is the demand?"

Once you have identified your product, you may need to give a face-lift or create a niche for yourself. Creating a niche is not an entirely necessary thing to do, as your manufacturer may already have adverts and jingles on television and other social media platforms. In case you want to go the extra mile, various tactics can be employed to increase the value of your products and carving a name in the market. For example, providing relevant and appealing information about a product will let the buyer know how having the product will fulfill their needs and provide a solution to their problems.

This information can be buyer guides, product descriptions, setup guides, video guides and comparison guides for products sold. Also, selling a range of goods with similar functions (e.g., hair cream, conditioner, moisturizer, etc.) will ensure a complementary variety of products. In the same vein, products that have many components and additional items are also preferable.

STEP 2; Contact A Manufacturer/Distributor

Once you have identified a high-demand product, the next step to take is to find a manufacturer, to set up the drop-shipping arrangement together.

Just like in the previous step, you need to do your research and consciously choose a manufacturer. The right research and information about manufacturers will help you avoid falling into the wrong hands and differentiate between legitimate manufacturers/distributors and fake ones.

One easy and fast way to know is the price of their goods. Usually, a distributor or manufacturer offers considerably better pricing, on varieties of goods/products that they offer. However, doing this may not be sufficient. Go a step further and study the supply chain of the manufacturer. The use of the supply chain network means you need to analyze who the manufacturer or distributors have been transacting with over time.

How do you get to determine real and genuine distributors? They would usually only negotiate with the retailer, and rarely with final consumers. Once you see a distributor who has a direct link with consumers, you need to be suspicious, they are most likely not manufacturers. Identify and contact a manufacturer that offers quality and variety of goods at the best price and who uses a good supply chain network.

STEP 3; Negotiate with The Manufacturer/Distributor

After contacting the manufacturer, you then get them to agree to drop-ship. Here, you get to discuss the price and seal the deal. Negotiation is very crucial in any business, and you need to be very careful regarding terms and conditions. Do not enter an agreement that you don't fully understand its terms and conditions. If you feel a deal is not so good, you can contact an expert who understands better. Also, make sure to enter agreements that are beneficial to you. Usually, the deal contains clauses like remuneration, return policy, shipping cost, etc.

However, in most case, the manufacturer may not agree to drop-ship. In this case, you need to look for an alternative. This usually requires locating a distributor. A distributor is a company that keeps an inventory of another company's product and disseminates the products to smaller companies. There are many ways to find a distributor. The best way is to find out from the manufacturer of the product. Another way to locate a distributor for a product is to surf related trade magazines and publications. Legitimate distributors can be found in online directories, at trade shows, etc.

After finding your distributor, you should note that before making a deal with them. it is necessary to obtain information on the handling of drop-shipping fee (if any), billing, and how they deal with product returns. In other words, be clear on agreements that relate to shipping bills, you don't want to be responsible for the shipping, or get caught in the web of the unfavourable return policy. As a matter of necessity, make sure to agree only to a deal that mandates the manufacturer to be accountable for the return of products either due to defect or wrong items.

STEP 4; Create an Online Store

After finding a company to drop-ship, the next step is to build the online shop and sales channel.

Creating a sales channel means constructing a business structure and building a web presence. The web presence can be built by making an online shop or using an available pre-existing channel. If possible, it is best to have an online store. That way, the retailer will have more control over the business. Also, the retailer will be able to avoid fees, customize the look and develop a vibrant relationship with clients and buyers. Building an online store will, however, require more time and commitment than using a sales channel. There will also be the need for a business name.

There are significant things to consider when creating a sales channel. First, there has to be a real business. Also, a domain name is important. More often than not, a domain name that sounds dependable, relevant, professional and easy to remember attracts more buyers. Web-hosting services provide domains. Also, a professional arrangement and setup of the website matters a lot. This includes listing products, detailed description, arranging for payment options and so on. Finally, the management of the website should also be considered. You might need to seek online tutorials or seek professional services of web developers to get this step right.

STEP 5; Market and Generate Traffic

The next step to consider is marketing and driving traffic. Marketing is done through product titles and product descriptions. Also, there are various online marketing methods to generate traffic. Some of them are blogs, social media (targeted Facebook ad, Instagram ad), free eBooks, email marketing, videos, and posters, participating in events and shows and so on. You might also need to take a course or two on this part to get it right.

Your website and the drop-shipping business is useless without traffic. You need to learn and utilize the effective methods of generating enough traffic to your online store before you can start singing melodious tunes because of how fat your bank account will become.

SECTION FIVE

The Pros and Cons of Drop-Shipping

I would not want you to be ignorant of the challenges that you may face in this business, but I will also add that the benefits outweigh the problems in many ways than one.

The Pros of Drop-shipping

Reduced/Eliminated Costs of Start-Up

The cost of shipping and building inventory is eliminated. Therefore, there is only a tiny amount of operating expenses needed. This is the most significant advantage that drop-shipping has over the standard retail model. As a result, no inventory means no leftovers. If the product being sold by the business becomes untrendy and worthless, your business has nothing to lose. You only move on to the next *in-thing*. Ultimately, forced discounts and slashed prices on old products to sell them off will not occur.

Less Physical Requirements and Actions

The struggle of finding a retail space and storage is eliminated in drop-shipping. Also, the stress involved in shipping, inventory tracking, returns handling, inbound shipments and managing stock does not exist. Additional expansion of product range does not translate to more work. The manufacturer or distributor are the ones to do all the necessary work. Likewise, as long as communication exists with the suppliers and customers, the business can be managed from any location easily.

Other Pros

There is the opportunity to always have new and trendy products on the website as soon as they are manufactured. A wide array of products can also be supplied to customers.

As earlier stated, regardless of these advantages, drop-shipping also has its cons.

The Cons of Drop-shipping

High Competition

Chief among the challenges is the competition involved in it. Due to this, there are lower margins. This means that other competitors may be selling their goods at the lowest prices possible to make a sale, although their profits may be little. This likewise applies to the drop-shipper. To compete, prices have to be lowered, thus lowering earnings on individual sales. Having good feedback and an attractive website but with higher rates may not bring customers.

Full Dependence on the Suppliers to Always Deliver

The drop-shipper has to rely on manufacturers and distributors to supply inventory. This may present the problem of accuracy of available stock and be unable to provide the advertised products. This happens if there is no synchronization between the business inventory and the supplier's inventory. In addition to inventory issues on the part of manufacturers or distributors, there are some other issues on their part too. For instance, since they are in charge of packaging goods, there can be a counting error, the product can be damaged or poorly packaged. As the customer service provider, the drop-shipper has to absorb any fees resulting therein.

Working with Multiple Providers

Sometimes, drop shippers have to work with multiple providers. The problem comes in when a buyer orders multiple of a single product, being delivered by different suppliers. This can cost the buyer more regarding shipping and can lead to the drop-shipper losing the sale. Besides, some suppliers hike shipping fees and add it to the product fee.

Little or no Control over the Product Requirements

Finally, a drop-shipper is mostly detached from the business. This leaves the drop-shipper with little or no control. Whenever buyers prove unsatisfactory or unhappy about low-quality products, expensive shipping, poorly packaged or damaged goods and so on, the drop-shipper has to take the blame and find a solution to the problem.

Evidently, there is the good and bad to the drop-shipping business, as it is to any other business. However, with careful research and planning, a flourishing and lucrative drop-shipping business can be developed with little or no glitches at all.

CONCLUSION

Drop-shipping is an efficient way to get started in the online business world. It gives room for launching a business with minimal financial risk, experiments with new products and quickly enlarged business. Drop-shipping allows for time to promote the marketing, product development, and sales aspects of the business.

You have every reason to engage in this passive business and earn some extra cash to become financially independent!

Will you be considering your luck at this business? That's for you to decide, but on my part, it's been really nice teaching you.

Regards.

Printed in Great Britain
by Amazon